COLORFUL COLORADO RAILROADS
In The 1960's
By Ronald C. Hill

ACKNOWLEDGMENTS

The author wishes to express his enormous gratitude and appreciation to the extraordinarily talented F. Hol Wagner, Jr., who is responsible for the design of the entire book. Hol is justifiably famous for his authorship of THE COLORADO ROAD, UNION PACIFIC MOTIVE POWER REVIEW and the distinguished series of BURLINGTON NORTHERN ANNUALS which set the standard for all subsequent works of that nature. The author and the Colorado Railroad Museum are very much indebted to Hol for his superb creative endeavors on this and many other books — all provided to the museum by him on a voluntary basis. Additionally, the author wishes to thank R. H. Kindig and Richard A. Cooley for their invaluable assistance in helping to select the photos for publication in this volume and to Kathleen Murray, Marcia Hanson and R. H. Kindig for their expert proofreading and other suggestions. Finally, the author would indeed by remiss if he were not to mention some of the many friends with whom he photographed trains during the 1960's: dedicated and enthusiastic photographers such as F. Hol Wagner, Jr., R. H. Kindig, Dr. C. Paul Lake, Ross B. Grenard, Jr., William Marvel, Dr. James Calvert, William C. Jones, Dirk P. Ramsey, Wesley Haas, the late Kenneth C. Crist and many others. Without their knowledge and zeal, many of the images presented in this book would never have been captured.

PHOTOGRAPHY

All photographs are by the author. They were made with a Leica M-3, M-2 or M-4 camera on various different color transparency films, including Kodachrome, Kodachrome II, Kodachrome X, Ektachrome X and Agfachrome. The Kodachromes have stood the test of time best of all.

Title Page Photo: Three brand new GP40's roll an eastbound D&RGW hotshot downgrade through fresh snow below the mouth of Coal Creek Canyon on January 16, 1966.

Library of Congress Card Number 92-73251
ISBN Number 0-918654-45-9

Published by the Colorado Railroad Historical Foundation, Inc.
Colorado Railroad Museum
P.O. Box 10
Golden, Colorado 80402

Printed by Dai Nippon (Tokyo)
Tokyo, Japan

INTRODUCTION

In this all-color volume of Ron Hill's superior photography, we encounter engines and trains of the 1960's, at various locations around Colorado. Numerous railroads operated in the state, in the flatlands of the eastern part of the state, along the minor grades of the foothills, and in the rugged and spectacular scenery of the Rocky Mountains. Since no two railroads seemed to agree on color schemes or styles of lettering and numerals on their locomotives, they never have identical arrangements to present to the viewer. This diversity leads to a wide range of colorful and attractive opportunities for the railroad photographer, and Ron Hill has taken full advantage of the pictorial possibilities available.

Some railroads orginated or terminated in the state, while others merely passed through, enroute to other destinations. With the clear, sharp, and beautifully exposed pictures in this volume, we can see how railroad operations were conducted during this period. Some lines have modified or changed colors and lettering since these photographs were taken, while others, such as the Rock Island, have vanished completely. Therefore, a great many of the views can no longer be recorded just as they were when the photographer was busily compiling the pictures for this book, although many of the locations are still available for anyone who wishes to show more modern power at some of the places included here.

This is, therefore, not only an assemblage of colorful photos, but also a historic look at past Colorado railroading. I heartily commend it to all who enjoy seeing pictures of modern railroading.

— R. H. KINDIG
Denver, Colorado

BURLINGTON

Destined for Chicago on a wintry February 7, 1965, a CB&Q freight
powered by a quintet of GP35's and 30's accelerates through the
Denver Stockyards complex.

Nearing the end of its westward trek, the Burlington hotshot "CD" rolls across Sand Creek Junction in Commerce City on November 14, 1965.

Right on time, the first section of the CB&Q *Denver Zephyr,* above, approaches Sand Creek Junction on July 10, 1966. At the same spot a few days later, pool power from the D&RGW pulls the "CD" freight. The exchange of locomotives between the CB&Q and D&RGW is quite common during 1965 and 1966.

Crossing the Union Pacific tracks at Sand Creek Junction on July 24, 1966, an eastbound Burlington freight is propelled by eight Chinese red units with a high-nose SD24 on the point.

The popular overnight *Denver Zephyr* speeds through Derby on October 25, 1966, en route to Denver.

Two CB&Q freights, the first led by a new U28B, left, arrive at 38th Street Yard in Denver on April 8, 1967. F-units are uncommon on the "Q" in Colorado during the late 1960's, and it is an unexpected pleasure to find an F3 on the point of an eastward freight in Derby, below, on August 5, 1967.

Pennsy units were extremely rare on the Burlington Lines in Colorado, and it is highly unusual to see a quartet of Pennsylvania Railroad engines on the manifest "CD" as it hurries westward near Derby on August 5, 1967.

Running west over Colorado & Southern trackage near Broomfield, the CB&Q *Buckwheat* local passes Lower Church Lake on December 3, 1967. Mt. Evans, wearing a fresh mantle of snow, towers in the background of this exceptionally scenic location.

Two scenes from the CB&Q 23rd Street engine terminal in Denver on February 22, 1969: three units headed by F3 No. 160A, above, await their next assignment (the SD45 at the rear is wearing an experimental paint scheme in anticipation of the forthcoming Burlington Northern merger), while nearby the E-units, which have just delivered the *California Zephyr* from Chicago to Denver, below, proceed through the wash rack.

Autumn is in the air on November 6, 1969, as two CB&Q SD9's
and a very short train wait for orders in front of the old brick depot
at Akron.

COLORADO & SOUTHERN

Three immaculate Northern Pacific F3's, leased by the C&S to help
with the fall sugar beet rush, pose outside the historic old roundhouse
at Rice Yard in Denver on October 13, 1961.

The very last standard gauge steam locomotive used in regular revenue service on a Class 1 railroad in the United States was C&S Consolidation No. 641 which ran on the isolated C&S branch from Leadville to Climax as recently as October, 1962. Here, the heroic locomotive is seen at Leadville on a crisp, clear December 13, 1961, ready for another assault on Fremont Pass. Mt. Elbert and Mt. Massive, the two loftiest peaks in Colorado, rise dramatically behind the locomotive.

A long C&S freight, with F7's and F3's spliced by an SD9, rolls down Mason Street in Ft. Collins on June 8, 1962.

16

A heavy Colorado & Southern ore drag, powered by F7's and F3's, grinds slowly southward up the steep grade on the Joint Line at Greenland on October 24, 1965.

The queen of the Colorado & Southern passenger service was the fabled *Texas Zephyr*. Above, the train climbs toward Palmer Lake on the Joint Line at Spruce on October 24, 1965. Headed by E5A "Silver Pacer," below, the southbound *Texas Zephyr* makes a brief station stop at Colorado Springs on December 3, 1966.

Propelled by a lone SD9, a C&S local consisting of empty limestone gondolas threads its way up the desolate Owl Canyon Branch north of Ft. Collins on July 2, 1966.

A quartet of F7's leads a northward C&S freight into Pueblo on
January 21, 1967.

A sunny afternoon in late winter finds a C&S hotshot climbing southbound on the Joint Line at Larkspur on March 9, 1967. The lead unit is a Fort Worth & Denver F7A, and, as is frequent practice during this era, the four F-units are spliced by an SD9.

Three black SD9's coax a slow C&S freight southward along the
Joint Line through Sedalia on March 12, 1967.

22

Headed for Wyoming on July 15, 1967, four SD9's accelerate a
Colorado & Southern train through Utah Junction in Denver.

The Flatirons and the Front Range of the Colorado Rocky Mountains form a magnificent backdrop for C&S time freight #77 as it hastens north out of Boulder on November 11, 1967. The gondolas full of sugar beets will be switched out at Loveland for processing at the Great Western Sugar Co. plant.

A brand new U30C, above, leads C&S southbound train #78 at Louisville on July 20, 1968. Powered by two new U30C's and two old SD7's, train #77 emerges from a sag north of Boulder, right, on August 31, 1968.

Chinese red abounds as two U30C's and five SD's pull a 150-car
train past the Valmont power plant just east of Boulder on
September 1, 1968.

A fresh coat of snow blankets the ground on November 16, 1968, as C&S hotshot #77, powered by a U30C and three SD7's, above, heads north through Westminster. Street-running occurs in Longmont as well as Ft. Collins. C&S 77, right, is northbound in Longmont on January 26, 1969.

A smoggy Denver morning on February 1, 1969, discloses C&S #77
easing through Prospect Junction as a switcher works the adjacent track.

One of the most spectacular photo locations on the entire Colorado & Southern Railway is at Lower Church Lake, just east of Broomfield. Here, C&S manifest #77 dashes northward alongside the frozen lake on March 16, 1969, as Mt. Evans and the Front Range glisten in the distance.

Powered by a U28B, a GP30 and an SD9 borrowed from parent CB&Q, a C&S freight travels south along the Joint Line at Florida Avenue in Denver on March 22, 1969.

On March 23, 1969, C&S train #77 ambles through Denver Union
Station and passes Prospect Junction as it makes its way north. How
dramatically the Denver skyline will evolve in the years ahead!

31

A southbound C&S train growls around the shore of Palmer Lake on April 5, 1969. Palmer Lake, an artificial lake created by the D&RG as a source of water for its steam engines, marks the highest elevation reached by the Joint Line.

MISSOURI PACIFIC

Nearing the end of its westward trek to Denver, the Missouri Pacific *Colorado Eagle* approaches
Littleton behind a Texas & Pacific E8 on October 22, 1964.

A truncated Mopac *Colorado Eagle* hurries southward through Englewood on April 18, 1965.

A Missouri Pacific hotshot, left, races west near Boone on February 20, 1966. Just a few miles further down the line, below, the train exchanges motive power with an eastbound manifest which had been dispatched from Pueblo with D&RGW power in order to save terminal time. Now pulled by Mopac units, the eastbound takes the siding to meet the other train before rushing back to Kansas City.

Powered by a GP38 and three GP35's, a westbound manifest roars through North Avondale on January 21, 1967.

Resting at Pueblo between runs on April 18, 1967, a MOP GP38 and three GP35's sit next to a string of D&RGW motive power.

A Missouri Pacific local powered by a pair of GP18's rolls into
Pueblo during December, 1969.

RIO GRANDE

The D&RGW *Yampa Valley Mail* and UP *City of St. Louis* accelerate out of Denver Union Station simultaneously in the morning of May 18, 1962.

At Durango early in the morning of September 26, 1964, D&RGW narrow gauge K-28 No. 473 is prepared for an arduous day on the increasingly popular *Silverton Train*.

With a majestic Alco PA1 on the point, the D&RGW *Royal Gorge* heads south at Wolhurst on October 23, 1964. The three stainless steel cars on the rear of the train are from the CB&Q *Denver Zephyr* and are being transported between Denver and Colorado Springs pursuant to an agreement between the two railroads.

41

An exceptionally well-matched Rio Grande *Ski Train* is coming off the wye at Tabernash on March 7, 1965. It is heading up the line to Winter Park where it will wait until late afternoon to transport weary skiers back to Denver. The D&RGW has operated ski trains to Winter Park continuously since 1947.

On a beautiful winter day in March, 1965, the westbound *Yampa Valley Mail* rolls to a stop at the Steamboat Springs station. Devoid of the mail contract for two years now, the train is still affectionately known as the *Yampa Valley Mail*.

A startled deer scurries down the steep embankment to escape the westward D&RGW *Yampa Valley Mail* as it traverses precipitous Byers Canyon near Hot Sulphur Springs on March 9, 1965.

Pride of the Rio Grande, the celebrated *California Zephyr* climbs
west through Plainview on April 25, 1965. The entire length of the
immaculate stainless steel train is etched against the backdrop of the
Colorado Rocky Mountains.

45

Pulled by five GP35's, above, a westbound freight crosses
Coal Creek and climbs toward tunnel #1 on July 11, 1965.
Summer has arrived in Middle Park as an eastbound
D&RGW hotshot powered by four GP30's, right, hurries
through Fraser on June 29, 1965.

The *Prospector*, overnight train between Salt Lake City and Denver, descends the Front Range of the Rocky Mountains below Plainview, top, on July 11, 1965. Powered by a solid set of F7's, an eastward Rio Grande freight, bottom, waits patiently in the hole at Rocky for a succession of passenger trains on July 25, 1965.

An early morning summer storm is clearing as a D&RGW picnic special climbs west toward tunnel #1 on July 25, 1965. The train is bound for Hot Sulphur Springs.

Just as D&RGW engines were frequently seen on the CB&Q during 1965 and 1966 (see page 6), so CB&Q engines often plied D&RGW tracks. Here, a shiny Chinese red set of Burlington GP30's and 35's lead a hotshot descending the Moffat Road above Pinecliffe on August 1, 1965.

The northbound D&RGW *Royal Gorge* accelerates away from a brief stop at the old stone depot in Castle Rock on August 8, 1965.

Eastbound at Plainview, above, the *Prospector* eases downgrade on October 10, 1965. Later that same morning, the *California Zephyr,* right, winds westward between tunnels #2 and #3.

Winter wonderland at Winter Park! The *California Zephyr,* above, glides majestically through the pristine snowy landscape on November 13, 1965. In the afternoon, the *Yampa Valley Mail,* left, slows to a smooth stop at the Winter Park station.

Snow is falling at Plainview, above, as the Rio Grande *Ski Train* climbs toward Winter Park on January 16, 1966. Included in the long consist are five heavyweight Santa Fe chair cars. As a hotshot speeds westward on the mainline, the *Ski Train,* right, crawls into Crane spur at Winter Park on February 6, 1966, to await its afternoon departure. F7 No. 5731 had been the trailing unit when the train left Denver, but an accident at Tabernash broke the coupler and required the units to be turned around in order to couple to the train for the trip back to Denver.

Carrying the TOFC traffic which became common from 1964 until the train was discontinued in 1967, the *Prospector*, above, nears the eastern terminus of its overnight run as it hurries along below Leyden on May 14, 1966. A couple of hours later that morning, the westbound *California Zephyr*, right, climbs toward tunnel #1.

A westbound D&RGW hotshot powered by four new GP40's and a GP35 runs through East Portal and is just about to enter the 6.2-mile long Moffat Tunnel on June 5, 1966.

Waiting in the siding at Rocky on July 4, 1966, this eastbound Rio Grande drag freight from Phippsburg is powered by an SD9 and three F7's.

The famous *California Zephyr,* above, climbs westward alongside South Boulder Creek below Tolland on September 17, 1966. An hour later the same morning, the *Yampa Valley Mail,* left, rounds the curve below East Portal.

Its consist swollen by two extra cars, the westbound Rio Grande
Yampa Valley Mail crosses the mouth of Coal Creek Canyon on
November 13, 1966.

Led by a set of classic F7's, left, an eastbound Moffat drag from Phippsburg rounds the curve coming out of Rocky on June 12, 1967. With an abundance of F-units to handle an enlarged consist, the westbound *California Zephyr,* below, climbs through Plainview on July 1, 1967.

Viewed from the cab of the F7A leading the *Yampa Valley Mail*, an eastward Moffat freight waits patiently in the hole in Tolland on a sparkling December 16, 1967.

The eastbound *Yampa Valley Mail* rolls through a magnificent
wintertime setting at Radium on December 16, 1967.

Early morning sunshine glints off the flank of the *Ski Train* as it nears Sheridan Blvd. in Denver on its westward climb to Winter Park on January 18, 1969. Today the consist includes three C&S coaches as well as three ex-C&O dome coaches.

A GP9, which has obviously encountered snow on the tracks, and a
set of F7's lead a Moffat freight down out of the mountains at the
site of the old Coal Creek water tank on February 8, 1969.

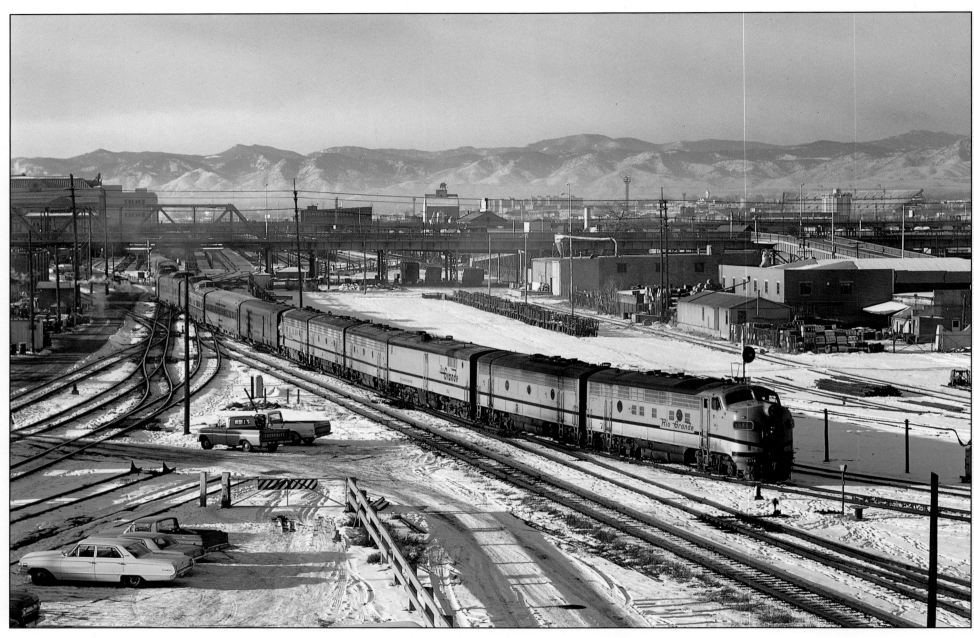

Fresh snow blankets the ground in December, 1969, as the elegant
Rio Grande *California Zephyr* pulls smoothly out of Denver Union
Station en route to Salt Lake City.

ROCK ISLAND

Three U25B's and three GP7's lead a Rock Island freight eastbound near Denver's Stapleton Airport on October 9, 1964. The Rock Island enjoys trackage rights over the Union Pacific between Sandown Junction in Denver and Limon.

The once-proud CRI&P *Rocky Mountain Rocket,* above, accelerates eastward at Sandown Junction on January 10, 1965. A typical Rock Island motive power consist, which includes GP18's, a GP7 and U25B's, right, is switching at Sandown on September 11, 1965.

An amazing assortment of diesels leads a westbound RI freight
toward North Yard from Sandown on January 9, 1966. The units are
an F2A, an FB1, a U25B and a GP35.

The Rock Island shared North Yard in Denver with the Rio Grande.
Here, an Alco FA1, which has been rebuilt with an EMD engine and
EMD trucks, basks in the afternoon sunshine at North Yard on
October 9, 1966.

The signal at Sandown Junction has turned green, and a light westbound CRI&P freight powered by only a GP18 and a GP9 accelerates into the small Rock Island yard on October 22, 1966. The north-south runway of Stapleton Airport bridges the tracks at the bottom of the hill.

Seen at Mesa, a Rock Island freight surges westward behind a U25B on October 23, 1966. During this era, the paint schemes on RI locomotives are almost never the same for all of the units in any given consist.

An empty Rock Island sugar beet extra led by a GP18 arrives at
Sandown on November 27, 1966, as Longs Peak towers in the
distance.

A Rock Island U28B leads an assortment of relatively modern
engines westbound into Sandown Junction late in the afternoon of
December 11, 1966.

The Rocky Mountains loom in the distance on May 7
1967, as an elderly CRI&P F2A heads up an
eastbound freight pulling out of Sandown Junction.

Viewed from the Colorado Blvd. overpass in Denver on July 18, 1967, below, this Rock Island train is traveling east behind a relatively new GP40. Another eastbound freight, right, is arriving at Sandown on August 5, 1967, behind three U28B's and two FA1's.

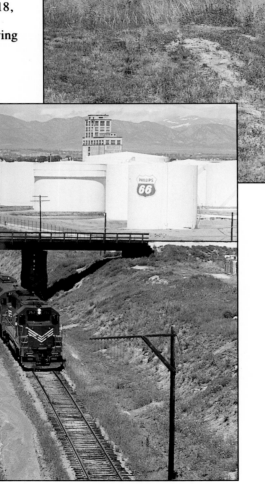

Still equipped with its original Alco trucks and prime mover, a classic CRI&P FA1 commands an eastward freight at Sandown Junction on April 7, 1968.

A trio of modern U33B's (but even these recent locomotives do not all wear the same paint scheme!)
pull an eastward freight through Belt on June 1, 1969. The Rock Island utilized the Northwestern
Terminal RR tracks to go from North Yard to Belt and then its own trackage from Belt to Sandown Junction.

Crimson and gray at Sandown Junction: A Cotton Belt SD45 and
Southern Pacific U33C and GP35 lead some Rock Island units with
an eastbound freight on June 8, 1969.

Bound for the flatlands, a Rock Island freight powered by a GP40
and three U25B's approaches Roydale on June 20, 1969. The
mountains are completely obscured by summertime haze.

Four aging GP's and a U28B make their way up to Sandown from
the west on September 13, 1969, with a short train.

SANTA FE

The Santa Fe owned more F-units than any other railroad. Here, four FT's wait patiently at the C&S
Rice Yard engine terminal in Denver on October 13, 1961. Soon they will transport a train south on the
Joint Line to Pueblo and then east to La Junta.

A southbound AT&SF freight pulled by a matched set of F7's growls
slowly through Sedalia as it makes its way down the Joint Line on
Christmas Day, 1963.

A veteran Alco RSD7 leads a consist of pure Alco power on a northward Santa Fe train coming around the curve into Palmer Lake on October 24, 1965. Alco locomotives are exceedingly rare on the Joint Line during this era.

Under the command of four F7's, an AT&SF freight charges westward near Boone, above, on February 20, 1966. An Alco RSD5, right, handles a work train near Avondale later that same morning.

Grinding slowly south on the Joint Line, four F7's are dragging a
long AT&SF train near Larkspur on December 29, 1966.

Nicknamed *Chico,* the short AT&SF passenger train which ran between La Junta and Denver scurries toward Pueblo at North Avondale, right, on January 21, 1967. On another day, below, *Chico* waits for passengers in Pueblo before heading up the Joint Line to Denver on February 2, 1967.

Three GP20's pull a southbound Santa Fe freight around Palmer
Lake on a dry winter day in February, 1967.

The air is crisp and cold during the early morning of March 9, 1967,
as a Baldwin switcher and an Alco RSD5 pose near the base of
Pike's Peak in Colorado Springs.

Two Alco RSD4's haul a Minnequa Turn through Pueblo Union Station on April 7, 1967, with ore en route to the nearby CF&I steel mill.

On August 5, 1967, a Santa Fe freight powered by a GP20, a U25B
and a GP30 rolls southward on weed-infested Joint Line trackage
near South Park Junction in Denver.

A matched set of AT&SF GP30's rushes a fast freight south at Wolhurst, on the Joint Line just south of Littleton, on August 6, 1967.

After new passenger locomotives were purchased for service on the premier Santa Fe trains, some of the old F7's suffer the indignity of handling freight trains such as this drag, above, southbound on the Joint Line at Acequia on October 22, 1967. Still led by F7's, the *Chief*, right, charges out of Lamar on an overcast May 9, 1968.

Three immaculate new Santa Fe SD39's stop at Rice Yard in Denver
on July 21, 1969, with a train from La Junta.

A northbound freight powered by F-units rolls to a stop in front of the classic AT&SF station in Colorado Springs on October 25, 1969. The pristine setting at the foot of the Rocky Mountains makes this arguably the most beautiful of any Santa Fe station.

UNION PACIFIC

An interesting assortment of engines reposes at the Union Pacific 40th Avenue engine terminal in Denver on October 18, 1964. At left is GP30 No. 844 whose arrival caused the renumbering of the famous UP Northern to No. 8444.

During the 1960's, variety is definitely the spice of life on the Union
Pacific! An Alco RS27, two GE U25B's and an EMD GP9 bask in
the autumn sunshine at Denver on November 1, 1964.

Two GP20's with a Union Pacific local wait in the siding at Sandown on May 1, 1965, as the eastbound Rock Island *Rocky Mountain Rocket* whizzes past.

For awhile during the mid 1960's, the Union Pacific routed the "KCLA," its hot Kansas City-to-Los Angeles manifest, via the Kansas Division through Denver in order to avoid congestion at North Platte. Here, the "KCLA" arrives at Sandown from Kansas City on December 5, 1965, behind two DD35A's and two GP30's. The top priority train usually rated super power such as DD35's and U50's.

Late in the afternoon of December 26, 1965, the UP "KCLA" speeds through Lucerne
on its frantic westward voyage. Two DD35's and two GP30's provide abundant power for the fast train.

The last rays of sunshine on January 30, 1966, illuminate a
westbound Union Pacific freight pulling up the grade into Sandown
behind a GP20 and two GP9's.

A bright spring morning finds the UP ''KCLA'' with two DD35's
hurrying west at 88th Avenue near Dupont on April 16, 1966.

Two Union Pacific passenger trains powered by E9's cross Sand Creek Junction during July, 1966: At left, the *City of Portland* leaves Denver headed west, and above, the *Portland Rose* arrives from Cheyenne behind mixed Milwaukee Road and UP units.

Accelerating away from Greeley, left, the UP *City of Portland* rushes toward Oregon on September 25, 1966. Powered by two DD35's and a GP30B, the ''KCLA,'' above, climbs out of the sag at Mesa on October 23, 1966.

Winter reflections: a crisp, clear January, 1967, day finds three
Union Pacific DD35's waiting for their next assignment at the 40th
Avenue engine terminal in Denver.

Boasting a U50, a DD35 and a GP30B, the Union Pacific
"KCLA" races across Sand Creek Junction during its
westward trek on April 9, 1967.

The last steam locomotive built for the Union Pacific, Northern No. 8444, steams through a photo run east of La Salle on April 23, 1967, during an excursion operated by the Intermountain Chapter, N.R.H.S. between Denver and Julesburg. Originally, the majestic engine bore No. 844, but it was renumbered in 1962 to avoid conflict with the GP30 shown on page 94. Eventually the Northern would regain its proper number following retirement of the GP30.

A solid block of Frisco diesels (GP35's and U25B's) handles an
eastbound Union Pacific freight at Julesburg on April 23, 1967.

The UP *Portland Rose* rushes eastward between Sandown and
Roydale on a sparkling Christmas Eve, 1967.

The new and the old: The first gigantic DDA40X "Centennial" unit, No. 6900, is displayed at Denver Union Station on May 24, 1969, to begin a new era of diesel super power on the Union Pacific. At right the equally immaculate UP 8444 approaches Sand Creek Junction on May 30, 1969, with a Rocky Mountain Railroad Club excursion headed for Laramie.

An interesting assortment of UP motive power, including a rebuilt F9Am (and a U.S. Army Alco MRS1) waits at the 23rd Street engine terminal in Denver on November 8, 1969. More than twenty years later, Coors Field, home of the Colorado Rockies, will be built on this site.

Dispatched from nearby La Salle, a UP local commanded by a GP30
and a GP9B switches at Milliken on November 15, 1969.

SHORTLINES

One of the most famous Decapods in North America, Great Western Railway No. 90, blasts up Oklahoma Hill near Loveland with a heavy load of sugar beets on December 27, 1961. When subsequently retired from sugar beet duty, the beautiful 2-10-0 went on to even greater fame on the Strasburg Railroad in Pennsylvania.

Homemade diesel No. D-500 of the Southern San Luis Valley
Railroad sits outside the dilapidated engine house at Blanca on
May 19, 1966.